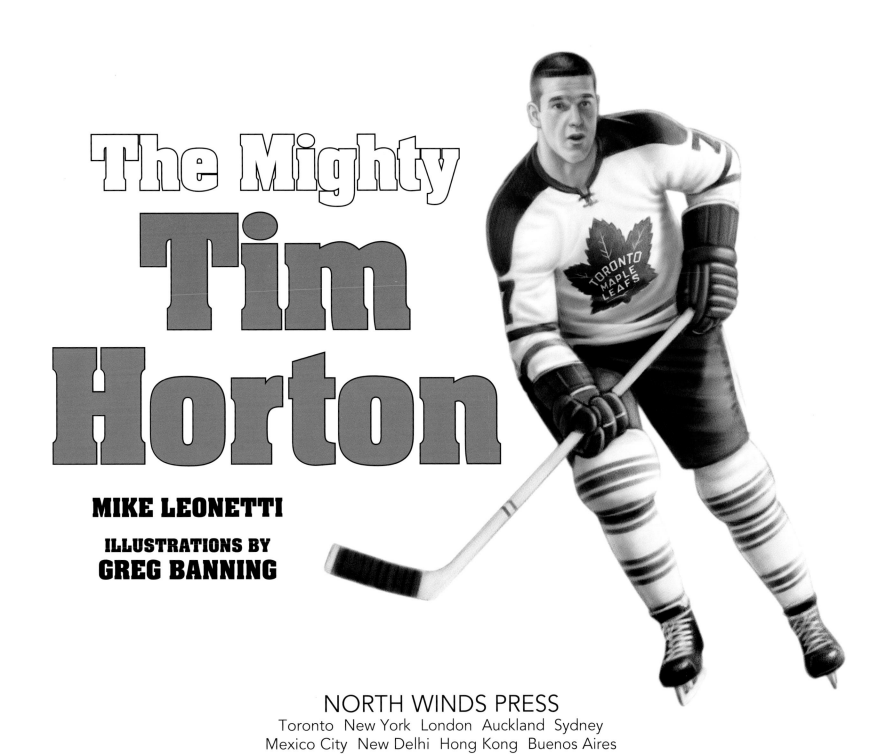

# The Mighty
# Tim
# Horton

**MIKE LEONETTI**

**ILLUSTRATIONS BY**
**GREG BANNING**

## NORTH WINDS PRESS
Toronto  New York  London  Auckland  Sydney
Mexico City  New Delhi  Hong Kong  Buenos Aires

ACKNOWLEDGEMENTS

The author would like to acknowledge and thank the writers and producers of the following sources: Books: Ron Buist, Charles Coleman, Tim Griggs, Lori Horton, Douglas Hunter, Ron Joyce, Craig MacInnis (Editor), Tom O'Driscoll (article), Andrew Podnieks, Don Weekes; Websites: Hockey Hall of Fame – the Legends, Wikipedia, The Canadian Encyclopedia (2007); Television and Video: *CBC Life and Times*, Stanley Cup film of 1962, *Hockey Night in Canada* 1962 finals games 1, 4, 5 and 6; Statistics and Record Books: *Maple Leafs Media Guide 1962*, *NHL Guide and Record Book*, *Total Hockey*, *Stanley Cup Playoffs Fact Guide*; Magazines: *Toronto Life*, *Hockey Illustrated*, *Hockey Pictorial*, Hockey News, *Weekend Magazine* (1973), Maple Leafs game programs; Newspapers: *Toronto Star*, *Globe and Mail*; Recorded Album: Let's Talk Hockey by the Toronto Maple Leafs.

While the events described and some of the characters in this book may be based on actual historical events and real people, Trevor is a fictional character, created by the author, and his story is a work of fiction.

Library and Archives Canada Cataloguing in Publication

Leonetti, Mike, 1958-
The mighty Tim Horton / Mike Leonetti ; illustrations by Greg Banning.

ISBN 978-1-4431-0042-7

1. Horton, Tim, 1930-1974--Juvenile fiction.
2. Hockey stories. I. Banning, Greg II. Title.

PS8573.E58734M44 2010    jC813'.54    C2010-901704-8

6  5  4  3  2  1        Printed in Singapore 46      10  11  12  13  14

To all those who love to play defense, and to Tim
Horton's daughters: Jeri-Lynn, Kim, Kelly and Traci.
—M.L.

For Marie and the girls, Flo and Meg. Thanks for
your love and support.
—G.B.

It was late in the game and the score was tied 2–2. As a defenseman I knew I had to keep the puck out of our end. I had a chance to sweep the puck away with my stick, but instead I leaped at the Terriers player, throwing him hard against the boards.

The ref blew the whistle. "Number 7, two minutes for charging!"

While I sat in the penalty box, the Terriers scored and won the game 3–2. I hung my head as I skated out of the box. I had cost my team the game.

Coach Regan pulled me aside after the game.

"Trevor, you took a needless penalty. And this isn't the first time. If you keep this up, there might not be room for you on the team," he said as he walked away. I stood alone, thinking about what I'd done.

I knew he was right. I was bigger than most of the boys in my league, and I liked to use my size. I had the most penalty minutes on our team. One time the coach even benched me for fighting.

I had to change. I loved hockey, and I really wanted to keep playing.

I thought about my favourite hockey player: Tim Horton of the Toronto Maple Leafs. He was a right-handed defenseman like me. Nobody ever got past him along the boards. And he had a great shot from the point. My dad said that Horton was the strongest player in the NHL and that he was never mean and never tried to hurt anyone. He'd averaged only one penalty minute per game in his NHL career.

"Maybe you should try playing more like him," my dad said as we got into the car.

I looked out the window as we drove home. I had heard that Horton lived near me. I always looked for him. I really hoped that one day I might see him and ask him for some tips.

It was two months into the season, and I was still spending too much time on the bench.

In December we had to raise money for our team jackets. Everyone had to sell five boxes of Christmas cards door-to-door. My dad drove me around to help me out. By the end of the day, I had just one more box of cards to sell.

"I'm tired, Dad," I said.

"Come on, Trevor. It's just one more," he said. "This will be the last street before we go home for dinner. I promise."

There was no answer at the first two houses I tried.
I decided to try one more.

When the door opened, I couldn't believe my eyes.

"Tim Horton!" I said.

He smiled. "Yes?"

I nervously said my speech about the cards and he
agreed to buy the last box. While he filled out my sheet,
I told him that I played defense on my school team. He
told me that was how he started playing hockey. I also
told him that I was mostly riding the bench, and asked
him if he had any tips for me.

"What's your name?" he asked me.

"Trevor, sir."

"Well Trevor, I'm going to give you a few pointers. If you follow them, it might get you playing more. Try to practise them every day," he said.

"Yes, sir," I said.

"And remember: it's okay to throw good, clean bodychecks. But I rarely fight. It really doesn't help your team much. That's why your coach wants you to have more control," he said.

"I think I understand," I said. "Thanks for your help, sir. I hope the Maple Leafs win the Cup this year."

"Me too. I've been waiting a long time," he said, smiling.

Before I left, he gave me four tips which I wrote on the back of my form. I couldn't believe it! Tips from Tim Horton!

I ran back to the car and told Dad what had happened.

"Now you've got advice from one of the best. I bet if you follow his advice you'll be a much better player," he said.

I read him the tips that Horton had given me.

"Number one: get the puck out of your end as quickly as possible;

"Number two: never look at the puck; play the man instead;

"Number three: make sure you have a good, low shot from the point, which is always directed on net to score or get a deflection; and

"Number four: practise skating backwards."

At practice the next day I told all the guys that I'd met Horton, but none of them believed me. It didn't matter. I just worked hard at being a better defenseman. First I worked on my backwards skating. And when I had a chance to shoot the puck, I tried to keep the shots low, almost along the ice. In my own end, I would take the puck straight up the ice or try to make a pass to a breaking teammate.

During the next few games, I wasn't all over the ice trying to hit every player. It was much more fun playing the Tim Horton way. I had fewer penalties, too. So Coach Regan started playing me more. Just two games later, I scored my first goal of the season!

Every Saturday night my family watched the Leafs on *Hockey Night in Canada*. But now I paid special attention to Tim Horton. Toronto finished in second place that season, and Horton led all defensemen with 10 goals. Only two other defensemen finished with more than Horton's 38 points during the regular season. I couldn't wait for the playoffs. I knew that Horton would lead the Leafs' attack from the blueline.

After beating the New York Rangers in the semi-finals, the Leafs were ready to play Chicago, the defending champions, for the Stanley Cup. The Leafs hadn't won the Cup in 11 years, so it wasn't going to be easy. My dad managed to get tickets to the fifth game at Maple Leaf Gardens. I really hoped the series would last that long!

At the same time, my team was ready to play the Hornets for first place in our league. I had gotten better thanks to Horton's advice, and I was looking forward to it.

We played a strong game. But with only five minutes left in the third period, we were tied 3–3. I made a clean hit on a Hornets attacker and picked up the loose puck from behind my net. I skated it out of our defensive zone and fed it to our winger as I crossed centre ice. I got in position to take a return pass, and he put the puck right on my stick. I skated over the blueline and made a move on their defenseman before letting go a low, hard drive to the far side of the net. My shot beat the goalie! My teammates jumped all over me. We hung on to win the game 4–3. We were the best team in the league!

Coach Regan smiled as I skated off the ice. "Nice shot, Trevor! That's the way to play," he said.

The Leafs won the first two games of the finals, but lost the next two games to Chicago on the road. That meant they'd be back in Toronto — I'd get to see a game at the Gardens for the very first time!

The night of the game, the Leafs scored within the first 20 seconds! By the end of the first period, the Leafs were ahead 2–1. Chicago scored two goals early in the second period to take the lead . . . but then Horton got going. First he took a shot that was going on net before it was tipped by Billy Harris and past goalie Glenn Hall. Just about a minute later, he took a pass from Dave Keon and let a hard shot go. It missed the net, but he followed up on the attack and got the puck back to Keon who put a shot high up over Hall's shoulder for another goal.

The Leafs ended up winning 8–4, and Horton got three assists. They were now just one game away from taking the Cup!

We played four games in a tournament over the weekend and won a couple of them. Even though we didn't win our division, I played well enough to be named a tournament all-star on defense.

Coach Regan talked to me after the last game.

"Trevor, I'm proud of you. You've really improved your game."

I smiled. "Thanks. And thank you for giving me more ice time. You know, Tim Horton's advice helped me a lot. He showed me how important it is to play hockey the right way."

We got home on Sunday night in time to watch the next Leafs game. It was still scoreless at the beginning of the third period. When Bobby Hull finally scored the first goal of the game, the Black Hawks fans erupted in cheers. But just a few minutes later, the Leafs tied it.

With a little more than six minutes to play in the game, the Leafs were on a power play. Horton took the puck straight up the ice. He passed it to captain George Armstrong who gave it back to Horton. Winger Dick Duff was open in the middle of the ice, and Horton got a pass over to him. Duff spun around and took a shot that beat Hall to give Toronto a 2–1 lead! Horton's assist was his 16th point of the playoffs, which set a record for defensemen.

Although the Black Hawks tried hard to tie it up, the Leafs kept the puck out of the net. Finally, the buzzer sounded. The Leafs were the 1962 Stanley Cup champions!

Two days later, my family went downtown to see the Stanley Cup parade. Thousands of people lined the streets, cheering. Many of the players were even signing autographs.

I spotted the car Horton was in and ran toward him with my Bee Hive photo of him. I shook his hand and asked him for an autograph. While he was signing, I reminded him of our meeting.

28

"How did my tips work out for you?" he asked.

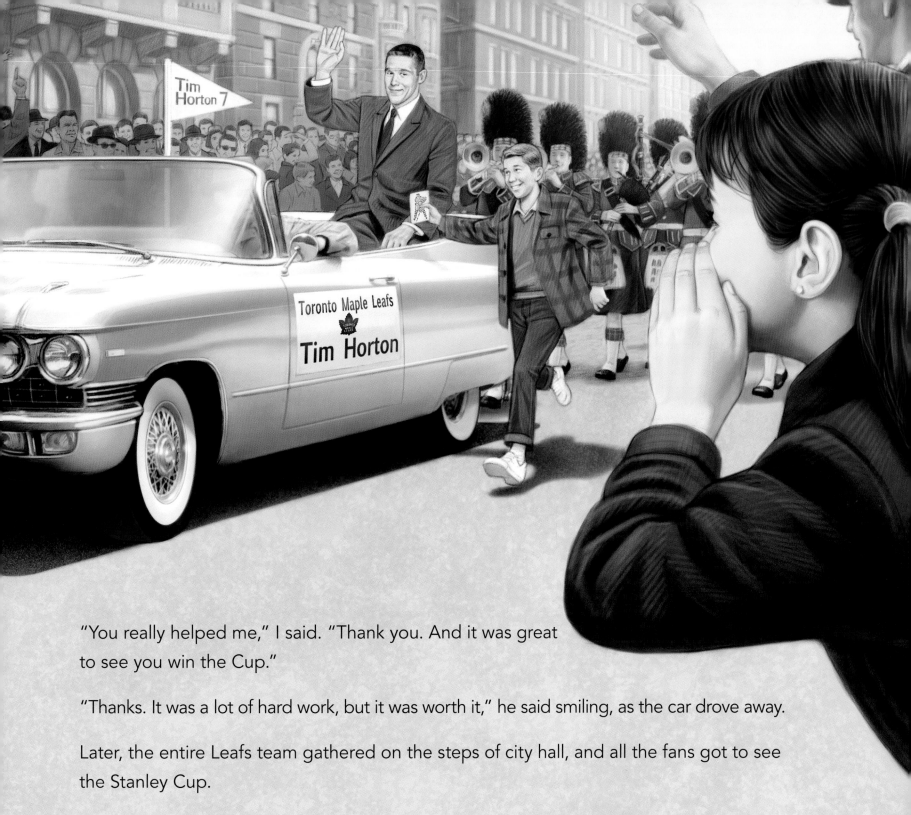

"You really helped me," I said. "Thank you. And it was great to see you win the Cup."

"Thanks. It was a lot of hard work, but it was worth it," he said smiling, as the car drove away.

Later, the entire Leafs team gathered on the steps of city hall, and all the fans got to see the Stanley Cup.

It was a moment I'd always remember. I could hardly wait until the start of the next hockey season.

29

## About Tim Horton

Miles Gilbert "Tim" Horton was born in Cochrane, Ontario on January 12, 1930. He started playing hockey at the age of five and by the time he was fifteen, he was a defenseman for the Copper Cliff Redmen, a team based in Sudbury, Ontario. His good play caught the eye of the scouts for the Toronto Maple Leafs, and that earned him a scholarship to St. Michael's College. Horton was named the most valuable player for St. Mike's twice, and the Leafs put him on their reserve list in 1947. He developed his skills with Pittsburgh in the American Hockey League for three seasons before he joined the Leafs for good in 1952-53. He suffered a broken leg and jaw in 1955 after he was hit with a bodycheck. Many thought his career might be over, but he persevered. Horton was the heart of the Leafs' defense for 18 full seasons and won four Stanley Cups with Toronto (1962, 1963, 1964 and 1967). He was named as an NHL first team All-Star three times (1964, 1968 and 1969) and earned second-team honours on three occasions (1954, 1963 and 1967).

He played a total of 1,185 games as a Leaf (including a team-record 486 consecutive games between February 11, 1961 and February 4, 1968), recording 109 goals and 458 points. Horton was traded to the New York Rangers in 1970 and would also play for the Pittsburgh Penguins and the Buffalo Sabres, bringing his games played total to 1,446. While he was still playing, Horton tried many business ideas and his notion to sell coffee and doughnuts proved to be the most successful. Today, Tim Hortons stores and other outlets are one of the most recognizable franchises across all of Canada. Horton was listed as the 43rd greatest hockey player of all time by the *Hockey News* in 1998 and he was ranked 59th on The Greatest Canadian list as compiled by CBC in 2004. Horton was named to the Hockey Hall of Fame in 1977, and his sweater number 7 was honoured by the Maple Leafs in 1995. He died in 1974 as a result of injuries suffered in a car accident.